# *A*PPETITES

## Alexander Dickow

MadHat Press
Asheville, North Carolina

MadHat Press
MadHat Incorporated
PO Box 8364, Asheville, NC 28814

Copyright © 2018 Alexander Dickow
All rights reserved

The Library of Congress has assigned
this edition a Control Number of
2018950273

ISBN 978-1-941196-74-8 (paperback)

Text by Alexander Dickow
Cover design by Marc Vincenz
Cover image from *Still Life with Herrings*
by Chaim Soutine, 1918

www.madhat-press.com

First Printing

# Appetites

# Table of Contents

| | |
|---|---|
| Grace | 1 |
| Go, little supper | 2 |
| The Banquet Unveiled | 3 |
| Famine | 4 |
| Appetites | 5 |
| Beverage | 7 |
| Abstract Meal | 9 |
| Meal | 10 |
| Three Still-lifes | 11 |
| Cabernet | 12 |
| A Kind of Fruit | 13 |
| Five Courses and a Digestif | 14 |
| Mess Hall | 15 |
| Dessert Recipe | 16 |
| Bulwark | 17 |
| Leak | 18 |
| Mob | 19 |
| Palanquin | 21 |
| Airlines | 23 |
| Ground Rules | 24 |
| Something | 25 |
| Far Afield | 26 |
| Minutes of Fruitless Search | 27 |
| Appearances | 28 |
| False Fronts | 29 |
| Open Secret | 30 |
| Two Human Movements | 31 |
| Breathblossom | 32 |
| Rain Parade | 33 |
| Fate | 34 |
| To a Politician | 35 |

| | |
|---|---:|
| Alternatives | 36 |
| Ascent | 38 |
| Descent | 39 |
| Crescendo dal niente | 40 |
| Diminuendo (morendo) | 41 |
| Drop Off | 42 |
| Poem | 43 |
| Woolgathering | 44 |
| Three for Paul Celan | 45 |
| Galaxy | 46 |
| After Turner | 47 |
| Overheard in a Far-off Language | 49 |
| Of All Things a Newborn Copy | 51 |
| Scenes in a Map | 52 |
| Breton Coast | 53 |
| Old Lithographed Landscape | 54 |
| Snow Colonists on the Palouse | 55 |
| Cityscape | 56 |
| Ice Storm at Freezeout Ridge, circa 1988 | 57 |
| Yardwork in Moscow, Idaho, circa 1988 | 59 |
| Maudlin Elegy in Lennox, Massachusetts | 60 |
| After Sappho | 62 |
| Love Poem | 63 |
| Love Poem | 64 |
| After the Song of Songs | 65 |
| Meditation | 66 |
| Putting Down the Head | 67 |
| Fragment of a Meditation | 68 |
| Emuna | 69 |
| | |
| *Acknowledgments* | 71 |
| *About the Author* | 72 |

תמיד תהלתו בפי:
**Ps. 34.2**

כל עמל האדם לפיהו וגם הנפש לא תמלא:
**Qo. 6.7**

# Grace

The best grace falters is true twice.
The stammer in conceit delights.
Wonder is a perfect drunkard.

*Alexander Dickow*

## Go, little supper

Go, little supper, and regale the timid
Hidden and unsteady. Preserve my sudden
Morsels from the rare gourmet: array
My many breath before the total connoisseur,
The all bouquet of men and women starved
For chord, or color, or companion.
Go, little supper, distribute you across
All longing, dwell before each thirst
My nimble spirits; gather up, provide,
Surrender and divide my bitter medleys,
My saffron scruples and my sweet remorse.

# The Banquet Unveiled

Its ripe urge spilt against the awe of guests,
Newborn and all crisp hope, an allegro
Gone and grown to the brim. A well-lit thirst
Thin in truth, a mere pageant in calm urns
And nests, foam arguing an appetite
Who beckons very tribes of an applause
And every hats remove upon the view.

*Alexander Dickow*

# Famine

How I have forgotten
Over my crown-blue hope,
Nor the green of my downy yearning,
The yellow of my whole ambition.
But I remember my famine,
How I was craved
By thirst blazing my brow
And aching my belly through,
Cut out and seized from fear.

## Appetites

One arm scooping the all sea
To drink my huge mouth of thirst
The other a mound pours
Each hungry bite of land upon
Never I have been so much
That my whole teeth eat
Upon the crackling of deserts
And sip teeming estuaries
In one lonely gulp.

Oh my archipelagos
Gnaw like nut clusters
While chew myself alive
The ocean trenches
And soon enough will nothing
Could remain minus
Spicy volcano

Reverie quenches within myself
While my gullet satisfies upon
Stinging honesty
Crunchy virtue.
Time for nosh on
Decorative blandishment
Colorwheels, equations:
The possibilities are
Everlasting.

*Alexander Dickow*

One arm swept about the total ocean
The other gathered
Each hungry bite of land away
Never I have been so much
Enough to drink my huge mouth of thirst
In one lonely gulp.

# Beverage

This tall verbiage
Whose fair inner blinks
While very foaming
Nimble much about—
I am weary so,
How it sweets
The every cockle
Without pause!

To drink it gives the notion
Stewed apricots taste with, it savors
Just a twinge bitter, it invites
A faint electric scent.

In it rounds out
Some of a structure oblique and haughty
Trembling with pinnacles
And clues.
By its crisp self-evidence it slakes;
Its plot unravels
Gently and perfect.

And I breathe up as I sip
the long progress
of a narrow in spite of far-reaching tickle
toward the spirit,
or like a creamy
and askew flutter,

*Alexander Dickow*

a muffled touching
rubbed with ecstasies.

# Abstract Meal

The concepts guests sip cups of
Quietly foam. Atop a bed
Of leafy quotients nest
The pungent conic sections.
Pass me a wedge of candied
Speculation. Who polished off
The tangy notion? Someone's
Picked every theorem off
The slanted frosting. The host
Ate too many symmetries.
What tasteful geometries!

*Alexander Dickow*

# Meal

Ripe eclipse with its omission
Fig reduction, sautéed intervals
With boundless crusts and round rinds,
Their hesitation contours, their icy brink
Fallen toward the palate refreshed.

# Three Still-Lifes

The door consents for slipping out
One taut suture of purity
That sleekly glows the workbench patchwork
Of crowded implements.
A stale broom stands slack,
A wig stranded on a stilt.

\*

Wallpaper in granny-pastoral:
Wildflowers all labeled in Latin, wildflowers
On a yellow field, wildflowers in bunches of
Wildflowers in quincunx, dainty wildflowers.

\*

Chardin's coarse cutting board
Warmly sleeps its rough-hewn loaves.
One cracked crust flaunts
Its foam crumb core.
The dull knife mottles
Beside the sharp cheese round.
They pleasingly resemble together.

*Alexander Dickow*

# CABERNET

This depth-tinted robe performs
Balmy and prolonging russets
And plum sparks.

Skillful while before or behind of the meal,
Vanquished over by too stark spice
As clove or cumin,
But blameless while consorting
Upon pointy cheese:

Pungent impish pinwheels sway the palate,
While swirl with characteristic somersaults
Overtoning the high redolence
Of ancient trapeze,

And all upon a slightly bitter finish.

# A Kind of Fruit

Faintly petal back the careful rind
eluding from the razor shrill
Of its outwardmost barbs.
Beneath it shrinks a wafered
Velvet envelope whose overlapping
Further skins you must shuck
Without remorse, only to surface,
Like vicious flesh that sheds
From the cruel health that's
Underneath, its bark: a husk crisp
And sparkled all upon with wanton luster.
Split that droplet splendor to release
Yourself a fruit whose frequent leaflets
Peel away a layered marrow, leaving
The pith around a core around its heart,
Around a stone, around a wish.

*Alexander Dickow*

# Five Courses and a Digestif

Timorous ranks of tidbit dumpling lumps

In dribble brine swim chunky nugget clumps

Biggest rack of gristle rib grub there is

Bespeckle flecks star the lettuce skirt fizz

More nectar syrup cluster glaze on cake

A fool will now a final liquor make

# Mess Hall

Swarms of chewy jaws
Eagerly gob whole quaffs
Of eatsome snacks
Amassed in vast slabs
And stacks of squat grips
Spew gropefuls of slather
And sour pours of swig
Between jagged cheeks
Down the biteful hatches
And the greasy sneers

*Alexander Dickow*

# Dessert Recipe

Stir throughout to thicken
The bulge, then whisk
To gradually involve
The luxury. Sprinkle chance
By generous coating.

Combine mixture,
Blend, and layer,
Then drizzle together.
Whip stiff peaks atop
Both dollops.

Up to completely melting,
Plunge slices within the ruffle
While creamy. Evenly spread
The accents and contours;
Fever in and out until firm.

Chill overnight.

# Bulwark

First signs will display slow ache against the seam
Soon following with faint agony toward the midst
Moistenings gather all surround the joints
Until thin steam inflicts the skin
Stress provokes to warping the morale
And the ribs to dangerously bulge
A puncture promises escape
Hisses
Sudden pegs propel and pounce among the vessel
Strain persuades a split between the heart
Venom serenades
The fissure desperate stopgap measures hush
For now

*Alexander Dickow*

## Leak

Between the porcelain the bucket lies upon
Where one by one I fall down in
And the high up plaster fissure
Plummets my perpetual birth
Each of me scarcely
As the fruit that squints between the husk
Each of me scarcely born
Burgeons loosens falls
And sinks below the somber bucket's surface
So I drown and I begin
Between the porcelain the bucket lies upon
And the high up plaster fissure
From which one
After the other
I fall.

# Mob

For a time being
I were milling free around
In faraway clumps.

There I am all splutter together in fountains,
Or peddling off on myself glossy trifles.

Close from the sandbox at which I am built
Castles, I would crank away the barrel organ
All along of which I fall a coin and two
Within my hat.

Some of me play chess.

At the fun-rigged
And many sparkled grind show
I was pleasantly divert of myself
Over impossible sideshow games
Padded up with tilted darts and thin decoys.
And I am snickering me and collected my loot
During I look wistful at my going away money.

And quick enough, alongside with the hook toss
A commotion was broken out
And soon I was all gang up on myself
Until I'm a narrow throng who gather up
To look the giant scuffle at.

*Alexander Dickow*

I cheer and I egged on me
Until I'm everyone join in.

Someday the dispute was dwindled
And weeping grievously
I would limp away
In triumphant glory.

# Palanquin

Forward, wicker throne!
Upon the squinting backs
Of my uneven lackeys,
Uprising the flagon
Of angry peace

And tilting this salute decree
To scatter hopscotch children
And to plummet over
Garden checkpoints,

Forward! staggering
Crown, you clamor tribute,
You prevail stiff bandits
And demand shiny onus.
Forward, retinue!

Upon my slanted knees,
Hoisting the jar
Of angry peace
And coughing howdy edicts
Against the jagged crowd.

Forward, wicker throne,
Careen me through
The debts and wishes
And gather me

*Alexander Dickow*

One still glass
Of easy time.

# Airlines

Overhead bins shall all carrion items
Engulf or underlurk the seat affront
Of you. Calm down now the every device.
Release a vise by raise the metal flap.

For floating you may use the cushion,
Your arms insert with straps until
Your heart against it hug.

And when the craft would come apart,
Adjust yourself the mask upon
Before insisting other passengers

And follow urgent lights who come alive
Until the hatchway most nearby
Unrolling where escape
Could slide undone into a desperate raft.

*Alexander Dickow*

# Ground Rules

Avoid to step the lawn upon,
Staying prior of the dotting lines.
Guard against your person
Your ticket at all the time.
Perform no litter,
Do not touch or otherwise
Tampering the viewings,
And there is no feed or pestering
With the animals.

During you found your seat,
Keep respectful towards
In speaking your neighbor:
Greet only with people
Among smooth diction.
Fail with the shouting or curse,
Nor jostle on themselves,
Neither disturb of their asleep babies.
Talk please and thank you always.
Wait upon your turn.

While the spectacle has completed,
Make your way an orderly
Fashion down the exit
From your left.

# Something

Here is something.
A hard mist resembling from everything
But isn't.
Cherish very fond with something
And cup itself among your vivid palm.
Surmise gently itself
As savage guesses in the dark.
Dip its muffled taste against yourself.
Contemplate over its visceral blur.
A variable stone. A compass
Whose map your distant body
Gives your unknown fingers.
Perhaps almost, yet
From whole practically purposes
Roughly, while just as smooth.
Precise between vicinities, or something
Else exclusively.
Look after something.
Tend for it and cup itself
Among your vivid palm:
For we are always touching
Something out of reach.

*Alexander Dickow*

# Far Afield

I whose stroll is go
Every most straightly
Toward these inclinations,
Whose steppings
Are formidable beeline
Under and above,
I who stoop tall!
I who tack astern
Dwindling mostward,
Whose detours
Harmoniously loop
Into the drifty wind,
I who weave straight
Into outright candor,
I know the way home.

# Minutes of fruitless search

Be it hereby noted
That in assortment color plastic containers
The discovery amount occurred was none.

Allow the evidence mention
That neither in casket or the cradle
Hunts are unyielding.

Let the record flourish
That the panoramas appear no clue
But thirst.

Henceforth concludes
All farther delving
Grows steadily absent.

*Alexander Dickow*

## Appearances

You see, the gift wrap already *is*
The gift: like God's names
Beautiful glossy over the mummies
Of our marvelous luck.

# False Fronts

Fillet the first of stucco thickenings
And rip back crusts of loss and hard ruin
For spy the clues which underneath display
In dim silks and shrewd veils who cloud the eye
Now shred away these vulnerable skins
And crackle upon the pale foundations
Until they flee along the useless seams
And falls away another aching slab
For show at last these startling façades
Like clustered explanations darkly grouped
Among the many page of weary books
These thin disguises turn them one by one
To innocence alone, and naked trust.

*Alexander Dickow*

# OPEN SECRET

I've got an idea
Behind my heart.
Either moment now
And I'll take my say:
I'll spill the breath,
I'll bring to wraps
An ace up one sleeve.

At any moment
I am hiding this
Candor outburst.
It's the question
For when. One minute
From the next, everything
Can turn on a
Direction, fall
On a tailspin, upturn
And lose out of hand
My heart on a sleeve.

# Two Human Movements

We describe the move inner
And the curl toward of scrolls and braids,
The inside shift, evolve and seethe
In shells and self and flesh,
The duck and coil of concept and clue,
The buckle down dust to no-win refuge,
The futile twist of return, wound-up
Surrender and desperate retreat,
The fist of a person;
Or we play the sortie, cast
About face and faith and feel, surface
And sputter ragged and pristine,
A compass push and pray or else
A lonely branching forward,
Whole thrust and thirst,
Drawn and in spun pursuit
A reckless come to light,
The fist of a person.

*Alexander Dickow*

# BREATHBLOSSOM

Wanes the grow blind bloom
In its dizzying high and
Ever far upwardness
Of grasp and gasp,
Down even against
Its nearest ache; swollen
From its nestle-born core
Whole of think and thrust
To its very tipmost kernel,
And all to its low fistful of grief
Spinning from hue to shade:
How it is that we all are
So beautifully swindled.

# Rain Parade

The long clouds fall
The million liquor down
The sky and into thirsts
So sweet to the touch
They burn.

And all this wise applause
Is quick to patience and to poise,
Like understated children
Dot across the drunken dusk
And disappear.

*Alexander Dickow*

# Fate

Before me is the past
Till I am born and now
I'll flee to my regret
The past is before me
In some future prison
Or in this garden future
Hands will hold me fast
Adrift in a sweet dread

# To a Politician

Your cellophane disguise for a tongue
Furiously unbefits the even knavest
Of these podium-fisted Catilines I hate
Whose dim broadcasts encrust
With craven abjectives and slick nouns,
Whose paramount pronouncements'
Weighty grovel fresh veneers each victim eye,
Who gape and crave at limp wealth,
Puppets of their own slanted lip
And their thin speech as cheap
As its callous stakes are ruthless:
Our brittle faith, our breath, the truth.

*Alexander Dickow*

## Alternatives

Behind the first door
Blacken coal abandonments apart
With which your heart will nowhere
Rest and fear,
Drifted wide by depths
And error loosening
Against the plunge
Where promises implore
Behind our breath and break
Faith, recede and plummet out of reach.

Behind the second door
Haunts a livid distance in between
Of where your doubts appear
And unappear,
Dwelled through with unsettlings
And with stinging qualms shrinking
From thresholds
Where crabbed utterings
Topple our blurred lips out
Into the numberless smoke and drown.

Behind the third door
Glares a jealous blaze beneath
From which your innards wane
And flee,
Stabbed over with fevers

APPETITES

And with rigid niches stricken
Crisp and even
Supple proverbs
Double back inside our mouths unsaid
To hide below the vacant clarity.

*Alexander Dickow*

## Ascent

Upper and more up upon the crest
So yearn we forth ourselves
Compelled full pinnacle above
Atop hills we rise over
Increased we clamber steps
And far encompass out these arms
Of hunger and horizon
We are grown high and heady
With sheer crescendo and beyond
Our upmost hope our home
We watch it rise our refuge
Out of reach

# Descent

Thus we dwindle back within
Our marrow native and below
Us reel and falter plunge
Our each defeat our every ruin
Fewer and less sound
Our downward pulse
Is reckless and surrender
Drowns the heart
And sorrow

*Alexander Dickow*

## Crescendo dal niente

Clues will lull the slow hush down
The narrow strain, an aria
Like intimations come to night
At first no louder than a scent

Though soon brighter than a drone
No paean, but a fierce defeat
A hazy stab in the dawn
More a murmur than a kiss

Yet just as desperate, a call
To rise deeper than the weather
Faster than the smallest number
Higher even than praise or war

# Diminuendo (morendo)

Hard proof has rolled the shrill cry up
To the vicious pitch of squalls
And shaken skiffs, a chiming out
At once more deafening than shame

Though soon less raucous than the sky
An anthem still, and dissonant
As flame's uneven unison
Less a conflict than a bloom

And just as frail, a whisper soon
To listen closer than the ear
Beneath the faintest hue, smaller
Even than silence, or the truth

*Alexander Dickow*

# Drop Off

Come fall awake together
Up this velvet drop off,
A steep tall nap to follow,
A hard act to overlook
And dizzy see the sea below
A yawning gulf to pit against
And rise, shining up and down
The rain, come win or loss
Through all our headlong daze,
Wide asleep upon a drowsy bluff,
Trusting too much ourselves.

# Poem

**1**

This craft is a rare vessel
Whose sands shift and slip
Through endless fissures.

Hourglass ships
Capsized lullabies
Themselves drift off.

**2**

Measureless oceans?
The lay of the land
Is no less tall a wager.

Here rise up bluffs
Faint and thin as hunger
A hard song to scale.

**3**

A thirst for sand
Swims to the mouth
And sings a sick ocean.

Illusion is a lust as fast
As the river never run
Over this bloodless bed.

*Alexander Dickow*

# Woolgathering

Eavesdroplets listen rhythmically
From clouds my ears are reckoning
Like sand the whelks asleep in opal flocks
Will one by one converse across
Their ocean tongues, marooned
Merino secrets in the lofty surf
Whose ebbing forward toward sleep
Strikes the sky, the roof, the shore.

# Three For Paul Celan

Oh tinge throated
Treble bird
Swallow
The color note song.

\*

Willow shade scented
Shadow tinted
Fish sorrow:
Downcast
Thin stranded line angles
Balance drown ballads
Upon the music sunken
Evening scales.

\*

The edge lipped
Tip hinted sliver
Ripples in the noon star
Sun stabbed
Center.

*Alexander Dickow*

# Galaxy

Measureless and vacant husks
Veneer along the pale gaps
Kissing the smooth-lit kernels
Far across the hesitation
Contours

Where cycles dip
Ebbing forth aromas
Of nectar vicinities
All gleamed among
Their dim stretchings

Remote surroundments
Hint around lucid cusps
And milk-blinkings swerve
Over grooved vastnesses
Whose lofty gazes
Empty to the brim resound

Finespun legions
Of distant stone pivot
Within strange rings
And innocent strains
Swivel endless and lilt
Like hearts wept upon
The rings of far-fetched motes
Tingling their ancient aubades

# After Turner

A color accompaniment promptly
Punctures with red and orange the gaze
At the heart of the canvas:
Yet the painter sifts this first affront
With fruitsome moods
That curb and soothe its borders.

These outskirts emerge a contrast
Verging on pale plunges to the left,
Nearly where a mournful landscape
Is appeared: palaces petalled and oblique,
Maternal lagoons, chalk bluffs pierced
From a fog bank over the distance,
All wilting steadily toward
The bouldered stretchings.

By way as a thicket, this crude wake
Of risen bristles backdrops reveries
In rich greens amidst greys at times leaden
And now fleeting, grasses stabbing with dusk.

A lone bright streak
Surrenders it all into resemblings of clouds
Tousled one by one in each direction,
The tracings imperceivable and curvious of groups
Rippling their dark- or milk-eyed wings,
Etched dim by night and nudity,
Flock of dust or patch of minnows.

*Alexander Dickow*

Each year it takes them
A century to come there
All the way from here.

# Overheard in a Far-off Language

Almost like unaware
Between its whole distances
Sidles a thin preamble.
With time from time the nude timbres
Soothe and slide and plunge so imperceptively…
But impulse more by more will risk among the pinnacles,
Even gently sharpening to tiny decrees
Before a pause untimely
Clusters with suspense.

By starts and spells the pattern plots
With occasionally calms crisscrossed
In spite the rarest waning ever so often,
To finally etch a high relief above stirrings and ruckus.

The rejoinder, counteryielding,
Denies with persistency next,
And fluttering rife mottos
Whichevery way possible

Prior of freshly happening some laughter,
Spare, even ridged laughter,
But pliably and slipshod,
Which, vanishing summations in mirage,
Loses me at last my track
Among the angled pirouettes
Of a far-off language,

*Alexander Dickow*

At once so alike from mine
Yet inscrutable so richly and so pure.

# Of All Things a Newborn Copy

This lower left-hand corner marks
The best of spot as any for begin
And let the canvas dazed and panic
Trace across my stinging brush
For spill precision over lines
Who cloud the edges' slender depths.

Nail down the stern line sorrow
Here, despite the foothold's dim
Along this crosshatched distance,
Where each mute outline severs
One another, where intersections
Blend apart like lips or lives.

Now upon I'm nearly through
This end, in spite where features
Not quite show (I'll fill the thinnest
Hints in after): a shy few contours
Left are waited for conclusion,
A final missing hue, a far cry.

And there's more enough aside
For further drawing out above
And boundless bare beyond
Whatever's now remained
Upon my raw and vivid sketch
Of all things a newborn copy.

*Alexander Dickow*

# Scenes in a Map
## Idyll

The merchant hawks
Crowb quarry's gelatinous stone
To the wispy mason leaning foreign
Elbows on a sturdy breeze and bargains.
Waterloaves rise in village ovens of Vepsc,
Frozen
Inland seas
Caravans wheel olives over
Waver.
Felt tip fens: tufts of rushes puncture strips of mud.
Vertical pencil ripples plot
The sky lichens of Isp.
Wayfarers clearing the tall pass through
Lofty inverted Vs listen
To the upper left corner
Of the ragged slice of butcher paper brush
Against a baseboard.

# Breton Coast

Seashells dart the grey dunes
Thin swallows fleck between
Slabs of surf and fences
Visitors splinter off
Rim the vacant gorse's
Low and strangled gambrel
A plaited vault crouching
Over furtive kingdoms.

*Alexander Dickow*

## Old Lithographed Landscape

A causeway wavers all the tilted days
Through hamlets ache and crouch the hills
A slow wharf dimly drinks the watery lake
Men lean their dugouts forward on a stilt
An unsound fog wafts of fish and founders
A long-ago dog neglects to bay

## Snow Colonists on the Palouse

The first white settlers were arrived
Along their flurries of hearsay—
Promises of frosty alcove
And savage rumors of profuse lands
Roaming with indigenous scatter peoples
Whose unwary riches for the plunder.

And soon enough the coils
Of processions entwined
And indistinguish from one another
The crisp families blur the wind and hills
Revolve like the color milk,
And a million crystal wagon wheels
Creak, and sway, and drift
Over the glitter and colorless slopes.

Since then from time to time
Some bright and broken
Arrowhead the native autumn
Leaves long ago behind
Still disappears beneath
The icy colonies.

*Alexander Dickow*

# CITYSCAPE

We bypass lunar windows
And the furious bumpy shacks;
Turning on their backs against us, stiff façades
Are sagging;
Here founder parched cement and stucco,
There brick and the soot would smear.
We are crossed at last the terse park
Of aloe and pines in bloom.

And it's a nestle of shanties
When corrugated steel and canvas, cinder blocks
Rummage together,
With branching out battens and slats,
Pitting by listless cardboard,
Spliced with fraying laces,
Some morassed in snarling garments.

There a parapet crumbling
Against amblyopic windowpanes;
While over there, concrete innuendos
Cavil in long trails of quibble.
Double-backed premises cling
One above another.

Here and there, a few pylons ruckus all the disarray.

# Ice Storm at Freezeout Ridge, circa 1988

And we arose
Always more highly up
Evermore more lifting
Atop the climb beyond
As far until the sinking undermost clouds
Would loom toward downward
And mountainous lofty mass
Surrounds around.

The thunder
Gradual accumulating occurred
Till once the building up storm
Had went at full sway and begun
At last we completely reached
Upon Freezeout Ridge.

The mosses and Artemisia
And so many another near herbs
Foam teeming and tiny sprout
In root tundra cities throughout
The sheen and sliver flesh
Of ice and sleet.

Ourselves wedged in the bending frost,
Soon unrooting and swept
Against any moment
The gale and over the valley canvas

*Alexander Dickow*

A boundless irresponsible art
Like the weather.

# Yardwork in Moscow, Idaho, circa 1988

A couple childs rubble bellyneath
A painstakenly autumn gather
And destruct it by cramble over
Or tossle them each other hairs
Take turns abathe in damp
Embalmy fragrancies
In the eager foreshadows
All emburied and final burst
Surprise
Or simple jump in instead
No mind a little slug and two
Enjoy the pillbugs roll up
Their pithy advice
Fall back
For get a good running start
And straggle across of the lawn
Lingering patches of resistance

*Alexander Dickow*

# Maudlin Elegy in Lennox, Massachusetts

Chasehews or fangloops and etcetera
Scatter in the backyard porch shed
The screen door of whose
Closed shut hard.
Mosquitoes wouldn't bite yet
During sunshine goes all over still.
Arch is the precise heart in the garden
At the folding-up table
Of a garden which frontier the overgrown green maples
With also green shrubs.
His eyebrows were overgrown and twinkle
And Jean smiled back.
Arch will overlook the dull lump up close
At a folding up table.
And he dabs a crimped rasp so a lump
Could look like the nose, hair, a chin.
Hello, my boy.
While Arch would speak, he can whistle his teeth.
Shrsso, my boy, shrssay now.
And Arch could play a conshrscertina.
Six in the morning sharp, Arch was always strolling down
The corner store and gets his newspaper.
I go sometimes with him to hold Arch's hand.
After, we walked on back the road having the newspaper.
Then the screen door will close shut hard.
From in a lawnchair Jean smiled in the garden.

APPETITES

His eyebrows smiled her back
During sunshine went all over still.

*Alexander Dickow*

# After Sappho

    for Annie

Sometimes as I draw near of you
My keen breath still hopes all at once
While throughout my blood glitters,
And my cheeks become maddening
As ripe heartbeats,
When a sudden dwindle pale as grass
Soon appalls my naked colors
As on the first day.

My hands are tottering, flicker
And wavered often,
And I sweat but I shiver
Like a little boy again
My tongue will
Turned to a very jumble
And frolics unexpectingly
As on the first day.

Sometimes as I draw near of you
I am whole fragile and strong
As on the first day.

# Love Poem

There is no praise above
The kiss my lips will be
For you, my beloved,
And that's a tall thirst,
A pipe dream long since slept
Against in slender hope.

There is no praise above
The kiss my lips will be
For you, my beloved,
And that's steep praise, a debt,
A warm hymn so quiet
Everyone will hear it.

There is no praise above
The kiss my lips will be.

*Alexander Dickow*

# Love Poem

It is an easy sentence: life
And all our lips have worn it smooth.
As a lily among thorns, so is my love.
It is an easy sentence,
And its foolish limbs swing raw
And naked as forgiveness
From the thin and tilted trellis
Of our distant mouths.

As a lily among thorns, so is my love:
Our folly, lust and loss
have worn it smooth.
It is an easy sentence, life,
A toy we throw against the garden
Of our distant mouths:
Bring them near again
In simplicity and faith.

# After the Song of Songs

Let me in, my sister, pure beloved:
The night is drip upon my every hairs
And my head astirs with dew.

                        Let me in,
My love: the wind is more blowing coldly,
Night is darken all of time more, and clouds
Disguise all over the so little moon.

Open to me, beloved, and we'll spin
Up to the bottom of the all-blue bowl
To lie and lie together like a proverb
Everywhere in God's mouth.

*Alexander Dickow*

# Meditation

We pass, yes, in a blink
Of the hand we pass straightwith
Out of laugh to mourn, and joys
We fall quick enough to patience;
Hard severities are soon
Burst into dance.

We pain for recalling
Delights of yesterday
During as much as we suffer,
And the adverse
Tells equally the truth.

# Putting Down the Head

Let us not fall into
The bitter fist of men,
But fall us, fall us down
Into Your countless hand,
Whole in clemency,
But not between the sudden
Fist of men. God, whole
In mercy, forgive and suffer
Me my plea: fall me open
In Your endless hand
And forgive my sins.

*Alexander Dickow*

# Fragment of a Meditation

My God,
Escape my mouth from evil,
And from my lips depart the lies.
Against ill will, let hush my soul;
Let myself resemble with the dust.
Untie my heart into Your Torah
And rise my soul within Your laws.

# Emuna

Again and again we've risen and run
Our rain wept lips against the same whisper,
Against another haggard weather in
The high hush of praise we've given over
And over and held out, our every hand
A still refrain, a hand woven in two;
And our windy hearts vaults broken into
Answers and hope beckoning to the land;
Again and again we've risen and run
Our rain wept lips against the same whisper.

# Acknowledgments

Thanks to the following publishers, media outlets and collaborators who have generously featured some of the poems herein: *The Forward;* the *Project for Innovative Poetry* and Douglas Messerli; *Poetry Quarterly; This Broken Shore* and Daniel Weeks; *Truck, Fieralingue* and Anny Ballardini; *Ekleksographia* and Amy King; Slowculture.eu and Marc Louis-Boyard; *Plume* and Daniel Lawless; Zackary Sholem Berger.

Thanks to Henri Droguet for his indefatigable support, friendship and encouragement.

Thanks to Annie for her sensitive, honest, and indispensable rereadings: you are, my beloved, my very first reader.

Thanks to my daughters, Eve and Margot, for being the poems you are.

# About the Author

ALEXANDER DICKOW was born in Lexington, Kentucky in 1979, and grew up in Moscow, Idaho. He now teaches French culture, language, and literature as an associate professor at Virginia Tech. As a poet, Dickow has published works in French and English: *Caramboles* (Argol Editions, 2008), *Trial Balloons* (Corrupt Press, 2012), and *Rhapsodie curieuse* (Louise Bottu, 2017). As a scholar, Dickow focuses especially on literature of the Belle Époque and World War I on the one hand, and on contemporary literature on the other; he has published many articles in French and English, along with two scholarly works: *Le Poète innombrable: Blaise Cendrars, Guillaume Apollinaire, Max Jacob* (Hermann, 2015), and *Jacob et le cinéma* (Nouvelles Éditions Jean-Michel Place, 2017). Translations from French include works by Gustave Roud (*Air of Solitude* followed by *Requiem*, Seagull Books, forthcoming), Henri Droguet (*Clatters*, Rain Taxi/Ohm Press, 2015), and Sylvie Kandé (PEN/Heim Translation fund grant project, 2018). Dickow maintains a professional website at http://www.alexdickow.net.

www.ingramcontent.com/pod-product-compliance
Lightning Source LLC
Chambersburg PA
CBHW031605110426
42742CB00037B/1277